POWER MARKETING
FOR
SMALL BUSINESS

How you can boost sales
with
low-cost video

Alfred Poor

TC — F — SB
The Center
for Small Business

December 2010

ISBN 978-0-9826526-4-0

Published by:
Desktop Wings Inc.
700 East Walnut Street
Perkasie, PA 18944
215-453-9312
www.desktopwings.com

POWER MARKETING FOR SMALL BUSINESS

How you can boost sales
with
low-cost video

Acknowledgements

I'd like to thank all the family, friends, and colleagues who patiently listened to me as I developed the themes and details of this book over the past year.

I also appreciate the time and effort put in by Bruce Brown, D'vorah Lansky, Robin Miller, and Anna Platz, who read through the early manuscript and made many helpful suggestions.

I want to thank James Malinchak and many of the people that I met at his wonderful Boot Camp event that helped me see a clear path for this project. It gave me the pieces I needed to get started.

I offer special appreciation to my friend, colleague, and mentor, Joe King, who has held my hand through this process, and who has probably forgotten—literally—more about marketing than I may ever know.

And finally, I want to thank my wife, Bebe, for her support and insight as she has watched me develop my various projects and careers over the years. I also am grateful for her careful eye in reading over the drafts of this book, which was greatly improved through her efforts.

Foreword

Maybe you're not a techie. Maybe you haven't fallen into the social media quagmire. Maybe you don't have "people" to "take your business to the top of Google". Most of that doesn't really matter.

What does matter is that getting new business is as important as it has always been and that many of the traditional marketing and advertising methods don't work as well as they used to. In fact, some are clearly going away. So what are you going to do about that?

One thing you probably *ought* to do is read this book by Alfred Poor: **Power Marketing for Small Business: How you can boost sales with low-cost video**. Alfred talks tech straight.

In clear English, Alfred lays out what's going wrong with traditional, ever-more costly marketing and advertising methods. (Can you say "Yellow Pages" and "print ads"?). He then makes an equally clear case for low-cost video as a method small businesses can use to economically jump ahead of the otherwise trivial and time-sucking "new marketing" methods. He helps you get right to something that works: low-cost video that will be watched and will work to build and solidify your business relationship with your clients and customers.

As Alfred writes, "It all boils down to this; in order to have a successful business, you have to have a successful relationship with your customers and your prospects." Video can help build those relationships and he explains why you needn't be a techie or even like technology (or use it yourself) to produce low-cost video to help your business.

If your business is winding down and you're about to head for the sailboat or golf course, feel safe to ignore the major shifts in marketing. If you intend keep and maybe build a small business, this book can help.

Bruce Brown

Quantum Results Coaching

Author of **31 Days to Relationship Marketing Mastery**

www.QuantumResultsCoaching.com

TABLE OF CONTENTS

POWER MARKETING FOR SMALL BUSINESS

INTRODUCTION:

DON'T JUST SIT THERE, DO SOMETHING

There's an old joke about business marketing:

Question: Do you know what happens when you don't advertise?

Answer: Nothing.

Okay, so it's not a real thigh-slapper perhaps, but it makes the point. If you don't have a marketing plan for your small business, you may not have a business for long.

The problem is that the world continues to change and the old rules don't work as well as they used to. In this new world of the Internet, wireless phones, and other new technology, everything is changing. And it's getting more and more difficult to get your message through to your customers, especially if you don't make adjustments to match the times.

I don't know if there ever *was* a time that you could sit back and let business just come to you. Aside from a few exceptions, however, you

1

now need to work harder than before to build your customer base. For many people, the recent recession has changed the question from "how do I attract new customers?" to the more essential "how do I keep the customers that I already have?"

Harness the Power

You need a sound and effective marketing plan in order to maintain and grow your business, especially in these times. But what does that mean?

In general, it means knowing what your business is about, so that you can convey the value of your goods or services to potential customers. You need to put your message out in front of as much of your prospective market as possible, to appeal to new prospects and to reinforce your position with existing customers.

For a typical small business with a market that draws on a local geographical area, it used to be so easy. Let's look at an example of how it used to be.

Fingers Not Walking Anymore

For example, consider the Yellow Pages. There was a time when every business and home had at least one telephone. And with each phone line, the phone company would deliver a new directory each year. Phone numbers are listed in the White Pages, and the business listings are in the Yellow Pages.

The Yellow Pages used to be the gold standard for local advertising for small business.

The Yellow Page listings are organized by categories, which can make it easy to find some products and services, but you may have to guess to find the right heading for others.

Today, however, the Yellow Pages books are just a shadow of their former selves. The latest one that I received is an emaciated ghost compared with past editions. They even went to pages that are about half the size of the original, presumably so that the book would still feel thick.

Phone books are shrinking, as shown by the new, smaller size of recent directories.

It's hard to find reliable statistics on the use of the Yellow Pages because many of the companies that track this information have a vested interest in the business. Here's an experiment that you can try on your own. Next time you're at a gathering, ask how many people remember using the Yellow Pages that day? ...that week? ...that month? I bet you'll find some people who haven't opened the book even once in the past year. It's clear that the Yellow Pages don't have the impact that they used to have.

In fact, if you look at Yellow Pages marketing these days, they often emphasize all the "extra" benefits you get with an ad listing, including online search listings. But who goes to the Yellow Pages online to search for a product or service? Google has a 72% share of the global search market (and 98% of the

4

mobile phone searches, according to one source); the Yellow Page search sites don't even show up in the statistics.

There's a recent development that could make matters worse for the Yellow Pages; phone companies want to stop distributing the White Pages (residential) directories. As I write this, the Pennsylvania Public Utility Commission has given Verizon permission starting in 2011 to only deliver the White Pages when requested by a customer. And the company hopes to make similar arrangements in New York, New Jersey, Delaware, and Florida.

I'm not saying that the Yellow Pages directory is dead, but it's got to be close to life support at this point. While it used to be the dependable (and easy) way to reach local shoppers, that's not the case anymore.

No More Fish Wrappers?

For an even more dramatic illustration of how things have changed, consider the typical local newspaper. Even some major cities have lost their newspapers in recent years. How bad is it? Consider this; according to the Newspaper Association of America, total print revenues in 2006 were a bit over $46 billion. For 2009, that figure dropped to less than $25 billion. That's more than a 45% drop in revenues. Wow!

Newspaper Advertising Revenues

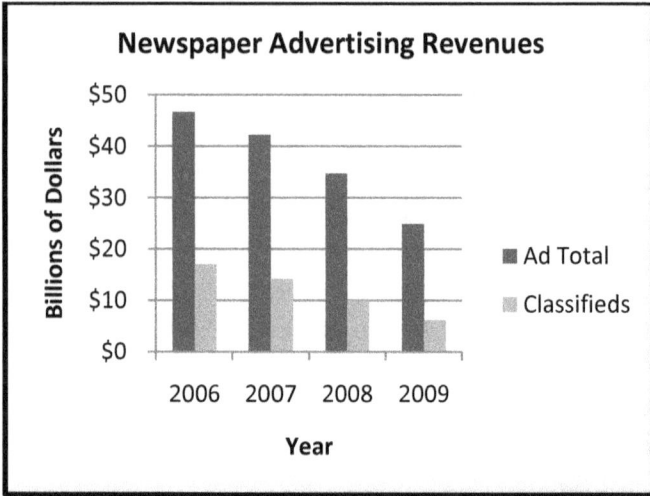

*Newspaper advertising revenues have plummeted
in recent years.*

But wait until you look at the revenues
for classified ads. They fell from almost $17
billion in 2006 to just over $6 billion in 2009.
That's about a 64% drop in revenue. Is it any
wonder that newspapers are in trouble?
Subscriptions are only a small part of their
balance sheet, and without ad revenues they
can't survive.

Newspapers used to be a dependable
cash cow, so what happened? First, we've gone
from a daily news cycle to an hourly news
cycle. By the time the newsprint lands on your
doorstep, you've probably already heard the top
stories a half dozen times. Who wants old
news?

But let's look at the classified section, if you can still find it. What happened to it? Once again, the Internet has changed everything. Why have a yard sale where only a few hundred people might see your stuff when you can sell it on eBay and reach millions of buyers? And you can get them bidding against each other so you are sure to get the best price. You don't have to sell that stack of old records for $.25 apiece only to find out that one was a collector's item worth ten times as much.

And then there's the Craigslist.com Web site. It's localized for specific geographical regions so that you can reach your local market. And in most cases, it costs you nothing to post a listing. The site includes want ads, job listings, real estate sales and rentals, items for sale, services, and even personals. Who needs the local newspaper anymore?

The Old Rules Still Apply

So if marketing your product or service in the local Yellow Pages or newspaper doesn't work anymore, then what the heck are you supposed to do?

I contend that the old rules still apply. I mean the really old school stuff. I'm talking about Dale Carnegie "How to Win Friends and Influence People" sort of things. It all boils down to this; in order to have a successful business, you have to have a successful relationship with your customers and your prospects.

These days, you may hear a lot of buzz about "Relationship Marketing" and "Social Networking" as if they are something new and revolutionary. While some of the tools and practices may be new, it's still the same old basics. Know your customer base and what they want. Reach out to them in a way that connects with them personally, and establish mutual trust and respect. Then deliver value reliably. That's still the way to build a lasting and successful business.

Okay, I'm the first to admit that this is easy to say, and somewhat more difficult to put into practice. Today's society is a bit different than it was in Carnegie's day. You can go years without getting to know your neighbor across the street. Our social circles are based on our work and activities and interests, and much less on geographical proximity. I have met people on the Internet—from across the country and even around the world—that have become good friends, even though we've never met face to face. On the other hand, I can't tell you the names of the family that lives across the street from me.

And with our busy schedules, it's hard to find time to meet new people and build new relationships. So it's not as easy to make friends and influence people in your target market these days as it may have been in the past.

So let's agree that it's not easy. I don't know of any magic switch that you can throw that will instantly grow your business and make you a success overnight.

And I also recognize that if you're part of a small business, you don't have a lot of time to put into new projects. You're probably like most people in the same situation, working hard and putting in the hours just trying to get all the essential tasks done. I understand that.

The Power of Online Video

But I also know this; you can add online video to your marketing plans and it can help grow your business by establishing a relationship with your customers and prospects. It can be more effective and more efficient than the alternatives. And you can do it without spending a lot of time and money. I understand that time and money are important because I get it that those are in short supply.

Let me be clear. I'm not talking about creating television commercials. They are expensive to produce and expensive to run, especially if you're going to run them enough to make them effective.

Instead, I'm talking about short videos that you can produce yourself and publish essentially for free.

As you'll discover in this book, you can create these videos at such a low cost that it may astonish you. And yet they can be powerful marketing tools for your product or service.

Even if you don't have any talent for public speaking or feel that you were born with "a face for radio", you can still use video to your advantage. As you'll find out in this book, you have many choices for the kind of content to use in a video. And I'll help you figure out which choices fit your needs the best.

What's in the Book

Here's what you'll find in the pages that follow. Feel free to skip around if you like, but it's not a long book and you may find it helps to just roll right through it.

In the first chapter, I briefly cover what it means to market a product or service in the new world of today. The goal is to create mind share (awareness of your business among your target market) to help you retain the customers you have now and attract new customers.

The second chapter talks about what "relationship marketing" means in this new world. I'll talk about some of the "hot topics" that you'll find in marketing books these days, such as Twitter and Facebook. Some of this is well-founded, but frankly I think some of it is snake oil.

Chapter Three covers how you reach people today. Online search has replaced the newspaper, Yellow Pages, and even the local community bulletin board. You don't need to become a Google expert to take advantage of this, but this chapter will pull back the curtain so you can get an overview of how the magic works and what you need to know about it. And you'll learn about what makes video such a powerful secret weapon for online search.

The next chapter lays out the advantages of online video for your business. Before I explain the "how" of online video, I want to make sure that you're solid on the "why". If you can't wait, you can just jump in at Chapter Four and see why online video is so simple and powerful.

Once you're convinced that this can make a big difference for your business, Chapter Five will show you how to get started. The key is to plan your message carefully, and I've made it easy for you to figure out what you want. You'll learn how the **PEACH** plan will help you focus your video content.

Chapter Six covers the ways that you can create your own videos, from hiring a professional service to doing it yourself. And I'll show you the third way that will save you weeks of time and hundreds of dollars (if not thousands of dollars).

You know what your message will be, and you have the means to produce a video. Chapter Seven will give you a step-by-step checklist to create your first video, including a number of key choices that you'll have to make along the way.

Once you have your video, you'll need to publish it. The next chapter gives you all you need to know to make the most of your video, from YouTube to your own company Web site.

Finally, Chapter Nine will help you plan to use video as an ongoing part of your marketing efforts. One video alone can be helpful, but this chapter will explain the benefits of a campaign with a series of related videos.

Do Something Now

I'm going to make a guess at this point. I bet that you're in business because you believe in your product or service, and you really want your customers to have it because you believe that it will make a difference for them. And I bet that you feel good when you help them. I know that's how I feel about my work.

And I'm going to make another guess. You are going to find that it's fun to make a low-cost video as part of your marketing program. You're going to have a good time doing this, and when you get to sit back and watch the final product, you're going to feel good about it. And when it helps you reach more customers, that's going to feel good, too.

The problem is that you won't ever get that finished video unless you actually start. So do yourself and your business a big favor; turn the page and dig in. It won't take long, and you'll soon be showing off your new video to family and friends. It's a powerful tool that will help boost your business.

So let's get started!

CHAPTER ONE:
MARKETING IN THE NEW WORLD

I t has been said that *marketing* is what you do to get customers to walk through your door, and *selling* is what you do to get them to give you their money.

This book is about the marketing part. My goal is to help you find your customers and prospects, and deliver a compelling message that gets them interested in your product or service.

Depending on your product or service, it may be that your business offers value, or dependability, or some other attribute that your customers and prospects seek. Maybe your message will include information that will help prospects qualify themselves; it's unlikely that your product or service is ideal for everyone. A good message can help prospects understand whether or not they are a good match for what you offer, which can reduce the number of unqualified leads that you have to handle.

Once you've got them in the door, the sales process is an essential but separate step. You can find lots of books and other resources on the subject of selling, but I'm not going to cover that here.

The Role of Marketing

I like to ask small business owners "How many members of your staff are involved in marketing?" Usually, I get answers along the lines of "We're too small a company; we don't have anyone doing marketing." At that point, I come back with *"Everyone* on your staff is involved in marketing."

Whether it's by design or by accident, everyone involved in your business is part of your marketing team. Every time you, or one of your employees, or one of your customers talks to someone else about your business, that's marketing. It's an important part of how people become aware of your product or service.

This goes on all the time, for better or worse. When you go to a party or other event and meet someone for the first time, I can just about guarantee that a question along the lines of "What do you do for a living?" will come up.

What many people don't realize is that this is not a marketing opportunity; it's a marketing event whether you like it or not. If you or your employee answers with a positive, enthusiastic response, that will help create a positive impression about your business for the other person. On the other hand, if you or your employee complains about some aspect of the business, that is going to create a negative impression.

15

The key point here is that you can either have a marketing program that leaves much of it to chance, or you can develop a marketing plan. It doesn't have to be an enormous project, but everyone in the company should be on the same page, making a concerted effort to deliver the same message to the world about your product or service.

Third Time's the Charm... Maybe

There's a classic concept in marketing. A consumer needs to be exposed to an offer at least three times before he or she will take action. Even "impulse buys" are often the result of repeated exposure to brand and product messages, which makes the item appealing when the right moment arises (such as when you're hungry and standing in the checkout line at the supermarket).

Unless you have an unlimited advertising budget, you can't be sure how your marketing efforts are going to get your message in front of a consumer the three or more times required to get them to act. So you need to make sure that you use the most cost-effective ways to broadcast your message.

Print ads and advertising in other media can be cost-effective methods, but don't forget the approaches that are either low-cost or no-cost.

One of these is to train everyone involved in your company how to convey your marketing message. What do they need to do this?

People often talk about "an elevator pitch". This is based on the idea that you step into an elevator, and discover your top prospect is standing there. You have 30 seconds to introduce yourself and make your pitch before you get off the elevator. Most people can't come up with something like that on the spot, so it pays to prepare something so you have it ready when the situation arises.

Your elevator pitch isn't just for your top prospect, however. If you have a clear message, that person you meet at the party is a prime candidate for the pitch. He or she may not be a prospect, but they are now armed with a succinct description of your business. If the situation arises in the future, they may be able to tell someone else about your product or service, and that person may turn out to be a prospect.

Your employees also should be trained in the elevator pitch. Make sure that they know the two or three most important points to tell people about your business, so that they can represent it positively and effectively when they talk to others.

And you can even train your customers to convey your marketing message. Make sure that any communication—in person or in writing—is consistent with your marketing message.

Mind Share

The goal of your marketing program is to gain mind share. When someone thinks of a certain type of product or service, you want that person to think of your business.

You establish and reinforce mind share by repetition of your marketing message. It's part of your brand, part of the overall impression that people have about your company.

By establishing mind share, you help retain your existing customers. And you attract new customers, because they will encounter the same consistent message about your company's product or service.

For example, you might have a dry cleaning business. Your message could be that you really care about your customers, and you want to make it easier for them to care for their clothes in the midst of their busy lives. As proof of this, you might mention that you're open early and late for commuters, or can send email reminders when their clothes are ready to be picked up.

Define Your Message

"If you don't know where you're going, you might wind up someplace else." You've put all this effort into building your business, and in many cases have developed a loyal customer base already, perhaps even without a coherent marketing plan. If you already have a plan that is working, that's great; video can be a powerful complement to your existing plan.

But if you haven't developed a clear marketing message yet, now would be a good time to start thinking about it. Even if you don't take advantage of the power of low-cost video marketing described in this book, a strong message will help you and everyone else involved in your business spread the word about what is so great about your company.

In the next chapter, I'll cover how you can make the most of your marketing message, by establishing a relationship with your customers and prospects.

CHAPTER TWO:
RELATIONSHIP MARKETING

A s I mentioned in the Introduction, the old ways are still the best ways. People keep putting old wine in new bottles, but in the end, the best way to have a successful business is to have a strong relationship with your customers.

What does this mean? I'm not saying that you have to be a close, personal friend with all your customers and prospects. That's just not a practical path for most businesses unless your pool of clients and prospects is tiny.

Instead, you need to make sure that when your customers and prospects interact with your business in any way, the contact helps build a positive relationship.

If your customers and prospects feel that they can trust your company, they will be more inclined to do business with you. You can help build trust through respect and friendly appreciation.

Building Trust

How, exactly, do you build trust?

There's no magic involved. Your customers encounter someone who is friendly, and who seems to care sincerely about how they feel and what they want. Your business delivers full value—or more—for the customers' purchases. And a promise made is a promise kept.

This is basic Small Business Marketing 101. It's easy to envision the traditional shopkeeper giving Mrs. Smith a friendly greeting as she walks into the store for her weekly purchase. Maybe there's even one of those little bells that jingles whenever the front door opens. And the shopkeeper always slips a little "something extra" in with Mrs. Smith's purchases.

Relationships in the Digital Age

Sure, that's a lovely Norman Rockwell scene, but how does it relate to today's world?

Each and every year, about one out of every six Americans moves. That number is much higher for young people in their 20s and for renters. (Of course, there's a big overlap for those two groups.)

The average American will move almost 12 times in his lifetime. Assuming an average life expectancy of 78 years, that means that they move every six and a half years, on average. No wonder it's so difficult to establish a relationship with your prospects and customers; they won't sit still long enough!

The mobile American society is nothing new, however. What is new is the way that communities are becoming redefined in the digital age. We have 500 channels of television programming that we can watch whenever we want, and if we're not satisfied with those choices, we have on-demand programming and DVD rentals to fill the screen.

If we can't find what we want to watch on television, there's always the computer and the endless Web to surf. No matter what our individual interests might be—from sports to hobbies to entertainment to politics—we can find a site that provides like-minded coverage of those topics.

When it comes to social interaction, we're no longer constrained to our immediate neighbors. Cell phones and email make it easy to maintain personal relationships with people across town or across the country. We don't have to make new friends; we can just keep in touch with the old ones no matter where we move.

Most people don't live in the same neighborhood where they work, so their colleagues are spread all over the place, too. In many cases, they'll never see the homes of most of their co-workers, even if they stay at the same job for a lifetime (which in itself is also unlikely).

How can a small business establish and maintain relationships with customers and prospects in such a disjointed and fragmented social environment?

The Online Emperor's Clothes

One of my favorite sayings is that "for every problem, no matter how difficult or impossible it may appear, there is always at least one simple solution... and it's usually wrong."

Some people believe that they have found a simple solution; use the same digital tools that have fragmented our communities to reach out to customers and prospects. In fact, you can't turn around without being bombarded with the opportunity to learn how to use "online social media" to grow your business.

You can find a host of workshops and a long list of books that will teach you how to make the most out of Twitter and Facebook to build your business. Build long lists of "friends" and "followers" who will spread your message and the new customers will flock to you. Or so the message goes.

I don't doubt that people have increased their bottom line through efforts using Twitter and Facebook and other online social media services. I am not yet convinced, however, that this is an efficient use of resources.

I suspect that a lot of these success stories started out with people who were enamored with the services in the first place, and then they spent lots of time getting to know how to work with it. And then they spent even more time building and maintaining the contacts that they establish there.

Now, if you enjoy doing this sort of thing, it's easy to discount the time you spend doing it. I saw the same phenomenon when personal computers first arrived. Some people would get a new computer and spend hours (or days or weeks) learning how to program them and then create programs to help them with their business.

Did these programs make the businesses more efficient? In many cases, they did. Was the return on the investment of time and effort worth it? In many cases, probably not. Had the person put the same amount of time and effort into building their business or making it more efficient using the old-fashioned, "boring" ways, they probably would have received greater returns.

So if you're fascinated by Facebook or Twitter, and simply want to spend lots of time exploring them and using them to establish new relationships with customers and prospects, be my guest. But be prepared to put a lot of time into it in order to get any noticeable return.

If there's one thing that the typical small business owner has in short supply, it's time. That's why I'm not convinced that "social media" is the most time-efficient way to grow your business.

The Numbers Game

Part of my problem with social media as a strategy is that it is difficult to target large numbers of customers or prospects using them. Let me give you a recent example.

JVC U.S.A. is not a small business. This is part of a multi-national corporation that had about $3.7 billion in revenues for 2009. The company distributes a wide range of consumer electronics products. So when they want to mount a marketing project, they have the resources to do it up in a big way.

Late in the summer of 2010, JVC U.S.A. launched a publicity campaign for some of its products. They used their Facebook site to run a daily giveaway program. Each day, they would put up a product as a prize, such as stereo headphones, a video camera, or an iPod docking station. The final prize was a 42" LCD HDTV, which is a pretty sweet prize.

To enter the contest, all you had to do was "Like" the product of the day. I guess the idea was that when you "Liked" the product, all your Facebook friends would see that you liked this JVC product, and it would make them think positively about it (as if you had recommended it).

I also suspect that JVC expected that like ripples in a pond, all this "liking" would get other Facebook members to "friend" JVC, and the contest would grow.

So the company gave away a prize every day for about seven weeks: about 50 prizes in all.

The first was a 19" LCD HDTV. And only 248 people "liked" it. That means that you would have had a one in 248 chance of winning if you were one of those who entered. Two days later, they gave away an iPod dock/CD player, and they got 1,001 people to "like" it.

By the end of seven weeks, however, they were only getting about 3,000 people to "like" the prizes. To me, that seems like a tiny number of entrants for a contest like this, especially when you're giving away a 42" LCD HDTV.

So in spite of the fact that Facebook has more than 500 million active users, JVC only managed to attract about 0.0006% of that number for their promotion, in spite of it running for seven weeks.

When I think of the money that the company spent for the prizes and the staff time to run the event (not to mention paying some creative agency for thinking it up in the first place), I have to wonder if this was the most efficient use of their resources.

My advice is to resist being swayed by the huge numbers being offered by some of these social media services, and instead focus on where your customers and prospects can be found most efficiently. Focus your efforts on how best to find them, and how they can find you. And that's exactly what we'll cover in the next chapter.

CHAPTER THREE:
THE KEY TO ONLINE: SEARCH

S o just how do you reach your customers and prospects in this modern age of a mobile population linked by digital communication?

As I described in the Introduction, the old ways of the Yellow Pages and local newspaper ads are not nearly as effective as they used to be. And there is every indication that they are in rapid decline. So what has taken its place?

The New Yellow Pages

Think for a moment about how *you* find a new source for a product or service. If you've got a computer (and most people do), chances are excellent that you turn to Google.

According to one source, users make more than 7 billion searches on Google.com every day. That's more than one search per day for every man, woman, and child alive on the Earth today.

In fact, online searches are so commonplace that the company name has become a verb; "I'll just Google it to find the answer."

28

People used to turn to the local newspaper and Yellow Pages to answer many of these questions. For example, say you wanted to find a pizza shop in Sellersville, Pennsylvania. Just Google "Sellersville PA", choose the Maps option, then use the "Search nearby" feature to search for "pizza", and you get something like this.

Google search makes it easy to find local resources.

You get a map of the area on your screen, with roads and points of interest clearly labeled. And there are digital "push pins" on the map showing the location of the various sites that matched your search, so you can see right away which ones are closer to you. (Try finding *that* information in the Yellow Pages!)

And if you click on a pin, you get expanded information about that one, including the address and phone number. You may also find user reviews, a picture of the location, and a link to the company's Web site. You can even get driving directions from your current location to the store.

Why would anyone use anything else to find a local business? This is quick, easy, accurate, and powerful. You get far more information than you ever could from the Yellow Pages or a newspaper ad, and you can get it customized to your individual needs in the bargain (such as the driving directions). Oh, and did I mention that this is all free to anyone with an Internet connection?

So how do you make the most of Google to promote *your* business?

Rank Has Its Privileges

If you do just a regular Web search for "pizza Sellersville PA", you get a list of Web sites for pizza restaurants in Sellersville. And like all lists, there is one inescapable fact; one restaurant has to be listed first. And that's a big deal.

Think about it for a minute. If you're shopping for something, you probably don't consider every possible alternative before you make your choice. If you're like most people, you choose between a few that you think will meet your needs.

And that's just what happens with Google searches. The higher you are on the list of the search results, the better your chances of getting the customer's business.

How much better are your chances? Here's a graph from a Web-based advertising company, Chitika. It shows the percentage of traffic that went to sites based on their position in a list of Google search results.

Percent of Traffic by Google Result
Based on a sample of 8.2 million impressions, May 2010 (Source: Chitika)

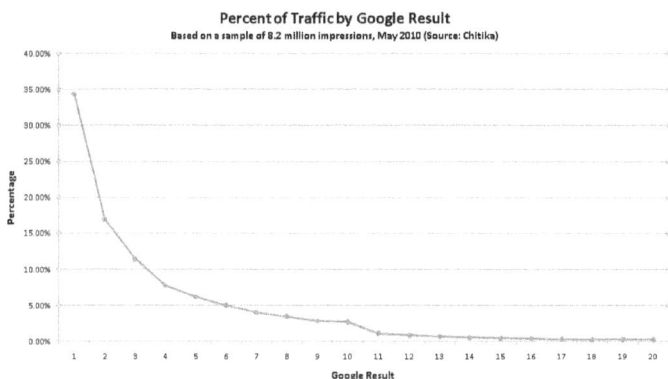

Traffic drops off rapidly as the search position gets lower.

According to these results, the top listing in a Google search gets nearly 35% of the traffic. Second place earns about 17%, or less than half as much. Third place gets 11%, fourth gets about 8%, and it drops by about a percentage point through the tenth position, and from then on everyone gets less than 1% of the traffic.

So the key take-away here is that when a customer or prospect searches for something to

31

do with your business, you want to be at the top of the list of results.

Search Engine Success

If you look, you can find lots of advice and books and seminars that will teach you how to get your Web site to rank higher on search results. You can also find companies that will do "search engine optimization"—SEO—on your site to improve its position.

Much of this is based on sound principles, though you have to be cautious about approaches that attempt to "game" the system, to trick the search engines into moving you higher on the list. In general, these tricks are short-lived, as the search engines find ways to spot them and remove them from their rating systems.

In fact, the New York Times recently had a story about an online company that discovered that bad customer service made people post complaints about the company on the Web. All these complaints caused the company's listing to jump to the top of the search results. Once Google found out about this, it developed ways to screen out negative mentions of a company, so that those would not be counted when determining the position in the search results.

The best SEO strategy remains the use of honest content on your site that will truly be a benefit for visitors seeking information on specific topics. This is often called the "organic" approach, and it will give you the best results over the long run.

So how do you create this good content, and how does it work? Certainly, this is a topic that could be the basis for an entire book—or even a series of books—but it boils down to three key concepts.

- Know your audience.
- Use keywords honestly.
- Keep adding content.

Here's more detail about these three concepts.

Know your audience

Know who you're trying to reach. If you're trying to sell pizza, then know what it is that people are looking for when trying to choose pizza. Don't try to dazzle them or baffle them with a lot of unrelated content, no matter how entertaining or informative it might be. That's not what they're looking for when searching for pizza.

This knowledge of your field is essential for the second concept.

Use keywords honestly

The way search engines like Google work is that they build a giant index of all the Web sites in the world. When someone types in a search on Google, it matches up those words in the search with the words it has found on all the Web sites. The sites that have a good match between their content and the search words will be listed higher on the list of the results.

Your task is to make sure that your Web site uses the terms that you think people will use when looking for a business or service like yours. So if you're selling pizza in Sellersville, Pennsylvania, then you better make sure that the words "pizza", "Sellersville", and "PA" show up at least once on your Web site. More times would be even better.

But you can't just create a page that says "pizza Sellersville PA" over and over a hundred times. The search engines are smart enough to recognize that, and your site won't get credit for those repetitions. In order for it to count, you need to have the keywords appear in a meaningful context. You want the information on your site to be helpful to visitors who come and read it.

By the same token, avoid the temptation to load up your Web site with everything including the kitchen sink. Again, if your business is focused on a particular geographical location—such as a pizza restaurant—then limit the place names on your Web site to a reasonable distance. People typically don't drive an hour just to get a pizza, so don't list all the towns in a 50-mile radius on your site. Concentrate on those in your area that provide most of your business.

Keep adding content

Don't let your Web site stagnate. The search engines know when you make changes to your site, and more active sites get listed higher on the results.

So consider what you can post on your Web site. Make sure the site is designed to make this easy to do, so that you don't have to spend a lot of time at it or pay a Web designer a lot of money to do it for you every time you want to add content to your site. One easy way is to add a "blog". This doesn't have to be a big deal, but it can be a way to share news about your product or service, offer discounts or special deals, and information about your business or industry in general.

Search Engine Extras

Also plan to take advantage of other free features available through Google. Remember those "push pins" on the pizza search earlier in this chapter? Those are part of the "Google

Places" service, and you can add an entry for your business for free.

List your company name and address, phone number, business hours, and your Web site if you have one. You can include a brief description of your business, your business category, or other information, and it's all free. When someone decides to "Search nearby" in your area for your product or service, your push pin will show up and your company will be listed in the results.

The Secret Weapon: Video

And now we're getting to the heart of this book's subject. You can use a secret weapon to boost your position in searches. And that secret weapon is online video. I'm not talking about commercials to broadcast over television; I'm talking about short video clips that are posted online.

Why is video so important? The answer lies in how Google treats it when considering where to put a Web site in the search results list.

First, Google favors sites that have video. Forrester Research did a study and found that sites with videos were 53 times more likely to be listed first on Google search results.

Next, Google indexes video clips based on a lot of information, including the title, description, and keyword tags. In the past, Google also has demonstrated software that can actually listen to the soundtrack of a video, and using speech recognition, extract keywords from the soundtrack to use when indexing the video for search.

It's not clear whether or not Google uses speech recognition technology in its ranking of sites, but it's still probably a good idea to use keywords in the spoken part of your video soundtrack, and display them on the screen as well if you can. This way, you can be sure to get the most advantage from having video on your site.

To recap this chapter, people are likely to look for your product or service using Google searches, whether they are looking for a worldwide company or someone local. Getting listed higher on the list of results more than doubles your chances of getting the business from that customer. And video is a way to help get your site listed higher in the search results.

The bottom line is that online video can be a compelling component in your small business marketing plans. And in the next chapter, I show you why it should be an essential part of your marketing.

CHAPTER FOUR:
ADVANTAGES OF ONLINE VIDEO

By this point, I hope that you agree with me that online video holds the power to transform your marketing efforts and help your business grow. In this chapter, I'm going to outline some of its advantages, but first, let me dispel some myths.

A company named TurnHere surveyed a bunch of companies of various sizes. Here are the two main reasons that companies gave to explain why they weren't using online video as part of their marketing:

- 67% said it was too expensive, and
- 33% couldn't see a clear return on the investment.

The first complaint just isn't true; good online video can be inexpensive to create. You don't need a huge budget and it does not take a lot of time, even to get professional results. I'll explain in more detail in Chapter Six, "How to Make a Video", but for now take my word that you don't need to spend a lot of money on this.

As for the other complaint—that it is difficult to see a return on investment—let me point out that just about any gain from a low cost investment is a huge return.

For example, do you tell your employees to smile when working with customers? (Okay, maybe there are some businesses where this might not be appropriate, but in general, smiling is a good thing.) What does that cost you? Maybe you spend a few minutes reminding staff to do it from time to time. Does this help retain business and attract new customers? Without a doubt. Can you track and measure the difference? It might be possible if you set up some complex split run experiment and tracking system, but frankly most small businesses don't have the time for that.

Instead, you implement some program—like reminding staff to smile—and over time you'll notice that things are going a little better. Or maybe a lot better.

I encourage you to track the impact of online video if you can find a simple way to do it, but just some qualitative probing may be all you need to know whether or not it is working. Ask your customers if they've seen the video, or just have your employees pay attention when a customer or prospect mentions your video. I have no doubt that you'll find that your small investment of time and money is generating a significant return.

So aside from costing less than you expect and providing a return on your investment, what are the other advantages of

online video as a marketing tool for your
business?

Quick to Produce

One key advantage is that videos are
quick to produce, especially when compared
with other forms of marketing. Consider a
magazine ad; you have to come up with the ad
idea, get a graphic artist to do the layout,
submit the ad to the magazine, and then wait
for it to be published. A newspaper can be a bit
faster because they are published more often,
but it still takes a fair amount of lead time.

With online video, however, it's nearly
instant. If you've got a new idea for a video
when you arrive at work, you could have it shot
within the hour, edited and ready to post a
couple hours after that, and posted online the
same day. If you push, you could have it all
done by lunch.

Sure, some ideas could take longer to set
up, shoot, and edit, but the point is that it's
really not a whole lot more difficult than
writing an email and just about as fast.

Repurpose the Content

You might think that creating a video is
not as cost-effective as making other kinds of
marketing material in print or other media. In
fact, it is just the opposite. Video is more
flexible and efficient than the alternatives,

simply because you can repurpose the material so easily.

For example, you can capture still frames from a video and use them as images for Web sites and print messages such as post cards and catalogs.

You can also get a transcript of the video soundtrack, and use the content as copy for printed promotional materials. If you have a video about a customer giving a testimonial, you can also use that same testimonial in print materials.

And the soundtrack itself can often be played without the images, either as is or with a bit of editing.

Video is even more flexible and efficient than some of the other choices for marketing materials because you can reuse the content in so many ways.

People Are Familiar with Video

There is something compelling about moving images. Perhaps it's the way our brains are wired, based on a prehistoric need to avoid getting eaten by some predator. But humans tend to be mesmerized by moving images: open flames, the ocean, and video. Why else would television and movies be so effective for story-telling?

People are familiar with video, and they are drawn to it. Now, I'm not going to say that they'll watch just anything that you put on a screen in front of them, but close to it. (I still have a hard time believing that some of the "stupid" commercials on TV go on to produce millions of dollars in sales, but it's a marketing fact.)

So people know what to do when they see video; sit back and watch. They know what it's about, and they're comfortable with that.

Video is Linear

One of the biggest advantages of video is that it's linear; you start at the beginning, run through the middle, all the way to the end.

Compare this with a pamphlet or magazine article. The reader can jump around, reading different parts out of sequence. They can skim the piece quickly, and possibly miss the point of important parts. And many people turn to the end first because they know that there will probably be a summary of the key points, and maybe they won't have to read the rest at all.

With video, it's difficult to impossible to speed read or jump around. As a result, you get to build your message so that it delivers your case as effectively as possible. And unlike reading a book where you have to perform an action in order to continue (such as turn the page), when watching video you only have to act if you *don't* want to continue. You have to actually do something to stop before you reach the end. If you do nothing, you watch it all the way through.

Now, it's true that some people cancel out of online video before they reach the end, but you're more likely to get someone to get your whole message using video than with text.

In the end, video is a powerful and effective medium that can be a flexible component that supports all aspects of your marketing efforts.

In the next chapter, I'll help you figure out just what you want to put in your video. I bet you'll discover that there are more choices than you might think.

CHAPTER FIVE:
WHAT TO PUT IN A VIDEO

What object has the most potential in all the world? A blank sheet of paper. It can become anything. It can hold an inspired business plan, or a beautiful work of art or poetry, or communicate a powerful message.

And it is this same unbounded potential that makes the blank sheet of paper so intimidating. Once you make a mark on it, you are committed to limiting what it could become. And that unlimited opportunity can be enough to prevent people from even starting.

It's one thing to say that you want to use online video, but it's an entirely different problem to come up with what you're going to say in it. What is your message, what do you hope to accomplish, what exactly do you want the video to do?

Don't Sell

As tempting as it might be to follow the examples that you've seen on television, resist the urge to make a sales pitch in your online videos. Instead, think back to the earlier chapters of this book. The goal is marketing, not sales. You want to get them in the door; once they've taken that step, then you can worry about selling them on your product or service.

So as I described earlier, you want to establish a relationship with the viewer. Create a feeling of trust and connection so that they get a positive reaction to your business. Be honest and respectful. That is the key to creating an effective message for your video.

I know, telling you what *not* to do is not much help. You need to know what you *should* do for your online video message.

The PEACH Principle

Like that blank sheet of paper, you can do just about anything with an online video. To help you structure your marketing message, I've come up with the acronym **PEACH** to help guide you.

Here's what **PEACH** stands for:

- **Position**
- **Educate**
- **Attach**
- **Compete**
- **Help**

Each of these represents a different focus for your message. It's rare for an online video not to include more than one element, but you should choose one to be the primary focus. This will make it easier to come up with the content and the design for your video.

Let's go through the acronym and discuss each element in some depth.

Position

A video with a Position message describes your business so that your customers and prospects know what you have to offer. No single product or service is ideal for everyone. It is important to be able to convey a clear idea of just who is a good match.

A key benefit of this marketing message is that your customers and prospects will qualify themselves. If your goal is to provide the best premium pizza with all-organic ingredients, that sends the message that your product is designed for a discerning customer base that is willing to pay extra for the quality (and the concept).

On the other hand, you may want to position your pizza as the best value available. You want to save your customers money, so you find the combinations that can produce a great tasting pizza at an affordable price.

Note that a positioning message focuses on your mission, your main goals for your customers, and the ways in which you want to do good things for them. This is all done without making comparisons with other companies. (That's a different message.) You leave it up to the consumers to make the comparisons, and to choose based on what they perceive to be the best match for their needs.

You want to make a strong statement about what makes your business great. And an honest, forthright presentation will help the viewer to see this as a believable message.

Educate

Another approach is to provide information. If you're willing to teach the consumer something about your business, something that they can use, they will see this as being a valuable gift. And in the spirit of "you have to give before you can get", being generous with your knowledge can be a great way to build goodwill.

One of the best types of education message is to take an aspect of your business that consumers might find confusing or intimidating. Sort through all the noise and give them an explanation that will help them make a buying decision.

For example, if you want to get a new roof, there are many different choices of shingles and roofing materials. How much difference does it really make whether you use the most or least expensive choice? What is the down side for spending less? Are there specific features that are essential, or that should be avoided at all costs?

Teaching the viewer to be a smart shopper helps build trust. By arming them with knowledge, they will feel more confident about making a good choice.

Another educational approach is to teach the customer or prospect how to do something for themselves, to help them save money. For example, it can be expensive to have a plumber come and repair a leaky kitchen faucet. If you would rather that your customers fix the little repairs themselves, and come to you for the bigger jobs, then create a video that shows how to change the cartridge in a kitchen faucet. The customers will appreciate your effort to help them save money, and they will still have the option to contact you if they decide that they'd rather have you take care of the repair.

Here's one key point: avoid the urge to cap off your message with a statement showing how your company's product or service is the only one that fits the requirements that you've taught through the video. This runs the risk of wiping out the benefits of the message, as the consumer will figure that it was all a setup to sell them on your business. And they'll start to question the accuracy of the information you've given them in the video.

Instead of seeing the information as a gift, they'll see it as suspect and question your motivation. And that's not a good way to build trust.

Attach

Why do some commercials use celebrities to endorse their products? Why do beer commercials often include shapely young women (who appear to have a very limited budget for clothing)?

The answer is that these ads want you, the consumer, to associate the product with these attractive people. And since you will want to be with these people, you will also want to use the advertiser's products so that you can be like these appealing people.

In short, the advertiser wants to attach their product to these attractive people, so that you have a positive opinion about their business.

Now, the chances are pretty slim that you've got a movie star living next door, so you may figure that your opportunities to attach your business to a celebrity are limited. But keep in mind that you don't need to attach your product or service to someone with a national or international reputation; they only have to be known within your market. And they don't even have to be known; like the girls in the beer commercials, they simply have to be people who are appealing to your customers and prospects.

How can you put this concept to use? Who do people talk about? In the fall of the year, the local high school football team gets a lot of attention in many communities. How could you use that fame to attach it to your business?

If you've got a pizza restaurant, why not offer a post-game pizza for free to the team, win or lose? Create a video of the happy players after a win, eating your pizza and celebrating their victory. You don't need to say anything else; people who eat pizza at your restaurant are happy winners!

There are lots of people in your community or market who are candidates for an Attach message video. Local elected officials can be good choices. And don't overlook the potential of existing customers or clients who aren't necessarily "famous". If they are well-liked or respected, and are the type of people that others would like to know, then a word-of-mouth endorsement by them on camera can be a powerful way to shape opinion about your business.

Compete

Okay, here is where you can draw comparisons. I don't recommend that you name your competition, but in this type of video you get to state what it is that makes your product or service unique, and that gives you an advantage over all other competitors.

For this to work, you need to have an advantage that is factual and credible, and it has to be perceived as an advantage by your customers and prospects.

For example, maybe you use a piece of equipment that is expensive or rare and that most of your competitors do not have. You can make the case that this helps you do a better quality job in less time, which is more convenient than other companies that take longer and may not produce as consistent results. Note that you don't have to say that it saves money; delivering more value in less time for the same money is still perceived as a bargain.

Or maybe you have a process or feature that sets you apart. If you don't have one, you can come up with one. For example, if you've ever built an outdoor deck for yourself or had someone do the work for you, I bet you can look around under the deck and find stray nails or screws that were dropped during the construction. Maybe you could get one of those magnetic sweepers, and say that before the job is finished, you will go around and make sure that any stray fasteners are picked up and removed. This will prevent children or pets getting injured by stepping on these sharp objects, or from other injury or damage when they are thrown by lawn maintenance equipment such as rotary lawnmowers or string trimmers.

It doesn't have to be much, but if you're in a business where your competition charges about the same for a similar product or service, you need to differentiate your offering. And a video can make a strong demonstration of what makes you a better choice.

Help

Customers and prospects like to know that your company is about more than just making a profit. Are you involved in the community? Share that through a video.

Maybe you sponsor a youth sports team. If you were to put up a video about the team, do you think the kids would want to see themselves on the computer? Do you think their parents would, too? And how many relatives, friends, neighbors, and co-workers do you think that they would tell about it? It's a natural word-of-mouth success story waiting to happen. And while it's about the kids and their team, your company gets credit for sponsoring them and providing support.

Or maybe you have a community service program where you contribute your products or services to non-profits or other deserving organizations. (And if you don't, maybe this could be a good time to start one.) A video highlighting your contributions would be of interest to a wide range of people in your community, and would be a topic of conversation that reflects positively on your company.

Also consider the efforts of your employees. Does one of them volunteer at the hospital, or with the local fire or ambulance service? Maybe one helps out at a senior citizen center, or serves on the board of a local civic group. If the individual is comfortable with the exposure, you can do a video profile of your employee. Not only does this demonstrate the generous contributions of the individual, but the company gets to share in the credit because it's the kind of place where someone like this would work.

So take credit for the good works that your company and your employees provide for the community. It will also enhance the reputation of everyone involved.

By now, I expect that you've got a list of possible topics for a video for your business. Use the PEACH Principle to help you think of a variety of stories that you can tell that will have an impact. And in the next chapter, I'll explain how to make those ideas a reality.

CHAPTER SIX:
HOW TO MAKE A VIDEO

For most people reading this book for the first time, I expect that the concept of creating an online video may seem like an overwhelming task. If you're not familiar with the process, you may feel that there is too much to learn and too many new skills to develop.

You may think that this sort of a project must take way too much time, or too much money, or both. I'll admit that you can spend a lot of these resources to create an online video, but the fact is that there are easy ways to save both time and money and still end up with a powerful result.

The Traditional Approach

The traditional way of producing a video—typically for a television commercial—is not that complicated. You go to an advertising agency and open your wallet.

These folks will handle the creative development, coming up with lots of concepts that are then presented to you, and then those get refined and worked up in detail. Then there's the script writing, the set design and construction, the on-screen talent, the camera operators and set crew, the editing, the sound track, and a host of other tasks that you never knew existed.

All this can set you back $10,000 to $100,000 or more for just a one-minute video. Granted, a five minute video won't cost much more to produce, but it's still expensive.

You can now find low-cost, flat-rate outfits that use digital systems to automate much of the process and create videos for you, but these still can cost $1,000 to $4,000 per minute. I expect that this is still out of reach for many small businesses.

The DIY Alternative

At the other end of the spectrum, you can create your own video. Here are the elements that you may need or want to use: camera, lighting, microphone, video editing software, soundtrack, and sound editing software. Here are some details on these items:

Digital camera: If you have a digital camera that takes still photos and is less than two years old, it almost certainly will take video. In many cases, it may even be able to record in high definition. The optics may not be the best, and you may be limited for some functions—such as zoom—but it can do the job.

If you don't have a camera, you can spend anywhere from $100 to $600 for a still camera that can do a decent job of recording video for you. If you want to get a camera designed for shooting video, expect to spend between $100 and $1,200 for a high definition model.

Note that you don't even have to shoot video if you don't want. You can just use still photos, and use a program like Photo Story by Microsoft (a free program) to pan and scan like Ken Burn's Civil War and baseball documentaries, and create an effective video without any live action video at all.

Lighting: If you want a raw, homemade look, you can just use the available lighting. For a more professional look, you'll want to control the light. You can get kits that include three lights with diffuser boxes for $300 to $500.

Microphone: If you're going to shoot someone speaking into the camera during the scene—as opposed to doing a voice-over—then you may want to be able to use a lavaliere microphone; make sure that the camera you use has a jack where you can plug in an external microphone.

Video editing software: Shoot your own video, and then use some editing software to clean up the video, add some title screens, and put it in the right format for uploading to YouTube or some other hosting service. Many versions of Windows include MovieMaker, and you can download it for free from Microsoft. It is not a difficult program to use, and you can learn the basics fairly quickly.

Soundtrack: Microsoft Movie Maker can even generate a looping soundtrack that will start and end with your clip. You can add voice-over yourself, recording with the microphone in a Web cam or built into a notebook computer. For $100 or less, you can also buy a good quality microphone that connects to your computer's USB port.

Audio editing software: You can also get free mixer programs that will allow you to improve the sound quality of your voice-over track. Audacity is one of the most popular programs of this sort, and it has many powerful effects including echo and volume normalization.

Add Up the Costs

For the traditional method, you will probably end up spending $5,000 to $10,000 for a five minute video clip. All the expertise will be provided for you, but you'll spend a fair amount of time working with the agency to develop the concept and refine the final product.

If you do it yourself, your out-of-pocket costs will range from nothing to about $3,000 (including a lighting kit and a good lavaliere mike), assuming that you already have a computer. Count on spending at least a few days to get to know your camera, video editing software, and audio editing software.

So you can spend a lot of money for the expertise and get all the help and skills that you need for hire. Or you can do it all yourself and complete the project for almost no expense. If you do it yourself and you do buy any equipment, it will be yours to keep and you won't have to pay for it again if you decide to do another video. (Which is something you'll probably want to do, as you'll see in the last chapter.)

No matter which approach you take, don't forget to include the cost of your time. Let's assume that your time is worth $50 an hour, just for argument's sake. Let's ignore the time required to choose an agency; maybe you've got a friend who can recommend one to you right off the bat. You'll probably still spend five to ten hours working with them on the details, which will add another $250 to $500 to your costs.

If you do it yourself, you'll have a lot of learning time required up front, in addition to shooting and editing the project. This could easily take 40 hours or more, which would be an additional cost of $2,000 or so. Once you have the skills down, however, you probably will be able to cut that time in half for future videos.

The Third Way

There's another way that falls in between these two approaches, and for many small business, it's a better way.

Look at the expenses of the other two approaches. The bulk of the expense is for the skills of shooting and editing the video. Either you pay a lot to the agency for this skill, or you invest a lot of your own time developing these skills on your own.

If you could get access to these skills in a more cost-effective way, then you could save a lot of time and money in producing your online video. And there's an easy way that you can do just that.

If you live near a city of any size at all, you probably have a wealth of videographers available. These people create everything from wedding videos to videos for business. And given that the cost of equipment and software is so low, the economic barrier to entry into the business is also very low. Competition is high, and you can find these services at prices that might surprise you.

In my case, I needed someone to shoot and produce a five-minute business video. This was to be a sample for a new project, and I had to keep costs to a minimum while still producing a video that looked professional (without appearing to be "too slick").

I turned to Craigslist.com, the online classified service where it costs nothing to post most ads. I posted a brief ad asking for a freelance videographer to produce a five-minute video, including shooting the video and then editing it, including the sound track.

Within three days, I had 18 responses (more than half of which came in during the first 24 hours after the ad appeared). I threw out the few "outliers" who were either way high or way low on the price, and was left with about fifteen candidates with most of the bids between $500 and $700.

I went to their Web sites and reviewed their portfolios of sample videos. (If they didn't have samples that I could view, I dropped them from the list.) I narrowed my list of finalists to about a half dozen.

At this point, my list included an Emmy award winner, a videographer who had worked with novelist Stephen King, one whose work had appeared on the Bravo network, and one who had created video for ESPN and Comcast SportsNet. Some had decades of experience, others were still college students.

In the end, I had my pick of several videographers, all of whom would probably have done an excellent job for me. The one I picked turned out to be exceptionally talented and skilled, and he produced a five-minute video for me for $500, complete.

So what did I have to do? I had to come up with the concept of the video, and the basics of what I wanted in terms of what would appear on camera. My project required that I deliver a scripted presentation, so I had to write (and rehearse) the script.

My total cash outlay was $500 for the videographer's services. I invested about half a day on the Craigslist.com ad and selecting the videographer. And I put a few hours into writing and practicing the script. We then spent about three hours shooting the five minute video. (Yes, I should have spent more time practicing the script!) So maybe I spent 10 hours total on getting the video made. Using my suggested $50 an hour for my time means that the total cost for my time was $500.

I used the same videographer for the next video so I didn't have to repeat the four hours spent on advertising and selecting the videographer.

So this third option meant that I had a $500 cash outlay and $500 time investment. And I had a finished video in just days.

For many small businesses, this approach will turn out to be the most attractive in terms of the cost: both time and money.

Note that there are other avenues that you can pursue to find a videographer besides Craiglist.com. As mentioned earlier, videographers often are hired for weddings, so inquire at banquet halls, churches, equipment rental companies, and other places that host weddings to see if they can recommend someone.

And there's another good place to find a videographer that you might not consider. Check with your local music store, especially one that caters to rock and roll bands. These groups routinely need videos to demonstrate their music, both as audition recordings and as a marketing tool to help sell their CDs. These groups often are scraping together what money they can for these projects, so they have to have cost-effective resources. As a result, videographers who work with bands will be familiar with making a three-to-five minute video, and can probably do it at a very affordable price.

Make Your Choice

Whether you decide to go the agency route, do it all yourself, or hire a videographer to handle the parts you don't know how to do, you'll have an avenue to getting your online video produced. As you've seen, it can be done for surprisingly little money and a minimal investment of your time.

Now all you have left to do is figure out just what you want to say and do in the video. The next chapter will walk you through all the steps you need to consider to create an online video that will do the job for you.

CHAPTER SEVEN:
PLANNING YOUR VIDEO

O kay. You're going to make an online video. That's easy to say, but harder to do. You could just pick up a camera and start shooting, but it is likely to turn out better if you have a plan. Where do you start?

The key to tackling any complex task is to make it manageable by breaking it down into separate steps. Here are the basics for planning your video:

- Choose your message.

- Storyboard (or outline) the video.

- Decide who will be on camera.

- Will it be scripted or spontaneous?

- Plan "B-roll" (or extra) content.

- Plan the editing process.

Let's go through these points one step at a time, and in the end, you'll have a good plan for your video.

Choose Your Message

One essential part of a good online video is that the content be able to stand alone. This means that it needs to tell a story or make a point all on its own. You can't count on the viewer reading a paragraph of explanation, or even the video title. Everything that the viewer needs to know has to be in the video.

Now, you can point the viewer to other places for more information, or what they need to do to respond to a call to action. But you don't want the viewer to finish watching the video and say "What the heck was *that* all about?"

Come up with the one message that you want to convey to the viewer. It has to be more than just "Eat at Joe's"; the goal is to build trust with the viewer and make a connection.

Go back to the PEACH Principle from Chapter Five, and build your message on one of these areas:

- Position
- Educate
- Attach
- Compete
- Help

Be sure to consider the audience that you're trying to reach with your message. Have the video tell a story or make a point that is relevant to them. Draw on everything you know about your customer base and prospects.

Storyboard the Video

The next step is to create a storyboard. This is a rough outline of the video, much like an outline that you would create for an article or report. You want to list the major points in sequence, which you can use as a guide when you shoot the video.

Don't be too concerned about getting it exactly right the first time. Just get your ideas down. You can revise them as you go along, and probably will.

A video is a visual creation, so your storyboard should have a visual component. You can find many different formats for storyboards online, but in general, you create an image and some text that explains the action or dialog that takes place at that point. (You'll find a sample storyboard format in the Appendix.) Use as many pages as you need to lay out the video.

This may be a bit intimidating, but think of it as a scratch pad for your ideas. Don't feel that you need to be a great artist. If you plan on having a title screen in the beginning, just write "Title" in the box and add some notes about the title and other information that you want on the screen.

For the scenes, you can make a sketch or just draw stick figures of what you envision. Can't draw stick figures? Then take a digital camera and shoot a couple pictures of what you have in mind. Just paste the photos on the storyboard and add your notes.

Item:	Date Of Shoot:	Location:	Page	Of

	Shot Number:
	Shot Type:
	Action/Script/ Detail:

	Shot Number:
	Shot Type:
	Action/Script/ Detail:

	Shot Number:
	Shot Type:
	Action/Script/ Detail:

	Shot Number:
	Shot Type:
	Action/Script/ Detail:

A sample storyboard template

As you're laying out your video, be sure to include key content early on. A study by the company TubeMogul found that about 10% of video viewers click away after the first 10 seconds, and more than half are gone by the end of the first minute. So make sure that you get part of your message across early, and then use the remainder of the video to reinforce that message in an engaging way to help keep your audience.

If you're using a videographer or agency to create your video, they can use your ideas as a starting point, and will probably have suggestions on ways to make the angles and composition more interesting. But you'll save them time by helping them understand how you see the structure of the video.

Some Planning Decisions

While you're working on the storyboard, you'll encounter a number of decisions that you must make along the way.

For example, one of the most fundamental decisions is who will be in front of the camera, if anyone. Perhaps you're a landscaper. You might want to do a video that shows off some of your work. You could do an entire video without any people in the shots, if you want, with a voice-over or text overlay to deliver a customer testimonial.

Or you could have a customer on-screen, talking about some aspect of your services that will deliver the message of the video. If you go this route, you could have the person just talking to the camera, or you could have them talking with you (or one of your company employees), or you could have them talking with a third-party interviewer.

There's no right or wrong answer to these questions, but you want to plan ahead so you know who needs to be there and what they're going to do.

You'll want to get signed releases from anyone who is included in your video. You may want to check with a lawyer to make sure that you've covered all the bases, but you can find all sorts of examples of a release on the Internet with a Google search. (I've also included a sample release in the Appendix at the back of this book that you can use as a starting point.)

You'll also need permission if you shoot your video someplace other than your property. Again, you can find examples on the Internet, (and I've included a sample release in the Appendix).

In a similar vein, you'll want to think about the dialog for your video. Are you going to have any talking, or will you just let text on the screen carry your message? If there will be talking, will it be scripted or spontaneous? If you're interviewing patrons of your restaurant as they leave, you'll want to make it spontaneous and capture their reactions about their meal. After you shoot a number of these videos, you can edit a bunch of the clips to create a compilation of rave reviews.

If you're going to write a script, the first point is that it may be shorter than you expect. You only need about 700 to 750 words to fill a five minute video, so you may find that you can't fit everything in that you want to say. Be prepared to work on the script and remove as much of the superfluous content as you can.

The other important point about a script is that it needs to come off as real and honest. If you're the person who will be delivering it— on or off camera—you'll need to practice it over and over until it becomes natural. If you're recording it off camera to be used as a voice over, then you'll have the advantage of being able to read from a printed script. You'll still need to rehearse it enough times that it doesn't sound like you're reading it. (Many people tend to fall into their "reading voice" when they start reading aloud, which sounds very different from their normal conversational voice.)

If you're going to be on camera, you probably won't want to be holding a sheet of notes if you want to be able to look at the camera or someone else in the scene. Here's a trick that may help you learn your lines with minimal effort. Just read your script aloud and record it. Then put that recording on an MP3 player or some other portable music device, and listen to it over and over. Listen during your commute to and from work, or wear earphones and listen to it as you walk around and do other tasks. In a short time, it will be stuck in your head like a top 40 hit, and you'll be able to deliver the lines smoothly and naturally when you get in front of the camera.

B-Roll Content

The least expensive way to create your online video is to use a single camera to shoot it. This requires half the equipment, and half the number of videographers that would be required for two cameras.

But just one fixed view of the scene may get monotonous, and zooming in and out or moving the camera around can be very distracting for the viewer.

You can avoid these problems and still use just one camera by shooting "B-roll" content. This is extra footage that can then be edited into the video at certain points.

For example, assume that you're showing the viewer a problem that often occurs with a car's cooling system. You can make one long shot where you're standing by a car with the hood open, pointing out key locations while you talk.

After you have that shot, you can then adjust the lighting and the camera, and take close-up footage of you pointing out the same spots. It can help if you recite the relevant parts of the script so that you keep the timing more or less the same, but you won't be using the sound from these shots.

Instead, the soundtrack from the original long shot will be used throughout the scene, and just the images of the close-ups will be edited in at the appropriate points.

Another example of B-roll footage would be for a landscaping business. While the main shot might be in front of your company headquarters, footage of client landscapes could be inserted in appropriate places. (Don't forget the location releases for those shots.)

This approach adds a lot of depth and interest to the video without adding to the shooting and production costs.

Prepare for Editing

You should make some other decisions before you start shooting because they will play an important role when you get to the editing stage.

For example, do you want any music in your video? If you have people talking in the soundtrack—either on or off camera—it can be a bit distracting to have music playing in the background. Music can be very helpful, however, to open and close the video.

First, the music can actually set the tone for the video that follows. If the message of the video is light-hearted and fun, then matching music will prepare the viewer for what is to follow. We've been well trained since birth by movies and television to pay attention to these musical cues, so you may want to take advantage of this powerful effect.

The music you use can also serve to brand your videos. This doesn't matter so much if you're only going to make one video, but if you are going to do a series, using the same music can help give them a unifying theme.

If you're going to use music, know that you can't just take your favorite hit record and use that. Copyright laws prevent you from using someone else's creation without their permission.

If you're using a videographer or agency, they can probably give you choices of royalty-free music tracks, or you can search with Google to find many sources. I have also had good luck with sites that post music by independent musicians—such as eFolk Music at www.efolkmusic.org—where I have found lots of good music of many different types. I have contacted the musicians, and they have been willing to license their music. In one case, I offered $50 for unlimited use of one track for a series of videos, and the musician was thrilled to have me use his music.

Another consideration is the question of text and graphics. You can create a title screen that looks like something that you'd get from the title feature built into a typical camcorder, or you can go all out with original art or a digital photo as the background for your title screen. In general, it's easy to take a typical still photo and use that in a video.

Take a photo and then use a graphics program like Google Picassa to add text to it, which you can then use as a title screen at the start or a credits screen at the end of your video.

As with the music, the graphics and text that you use in your video will set a tone and will help brand your video if it is part of a series. If there's a chance that you may do more than one video, you'll want to plan the text and graphics for the first one so that you can easily reuse them for future videos.

Make an Impression

Always keep in mind that you want to connect with your customers and prospects through your video. So you want to make sure that your presentation is consistent with the message that you want to convey.

For example, if you are an accountant, you might not want to create a goofy video or one showing a wild party scene. (Unless, of course, you want to create a reputation as the wild and crazy accountant guy.)

Throughout the process of planning your video, think about the overall impression that you want to make. Do you want the video to look like it was created by an amateur, or do you want it to have a slick and polished professional look? (Or do you want something in between those extremes?)

Again, there is no right answer to this question. In fact, a survey of YouTube viewers revealed that about one in five preferred video "produced by amateurs". Another 10% expressed an equal preference for amateur and professional videos. The best bet is to consider your target market, and decide whether they would be more open to a "homemade" video, or one with more polished production values.

One recommendation that I will make is that you plan on shooting your video in high definition, unless you're going for an old-fashioned look. The wide screen format and higher detail of high definition will look more current and timely, and is likely to make a better impression on the viewer. Most video hosting sites now accept 720p videos, so I recommend that you shoot your video at this resolution.

The key is to present your message clearly, in an honest and compelling way. This is the best way to make a connection with the viewer, and will be the key to building a relationship of trust between your company and its customers and prospects.

Put the Plan in Action

All that's left now is "lights, camera, action". Shoot and edit your video, and you'll be ready to publish it so people can view it. In the next chapter, you'll get some suggestions for easy ways to make your creation available to your audience.

CHAPTER EIGHT:
WHERE TO PUT YOUR VIDEO

Keep your eye on the prize. The goal of this exercise is not to create an online video, even though that might be a lot of fun. Don't lose track of the big picture; you're doing this to help your business grow.

You could just keep the video on your computer and invite people to come take a look at it, but you're not going to reach many people (especially not beyond your relatives and immediate neighbors).

You could put it on display in your place of business, but then the only people who would see it are your employees, your existing customers, and prospects who already know where to find you.

I'm not saying that you shouldn't do those first two things; in fact, they can be very effective in getting people to talk about your video and recommend it to others. But these methods won't reach many people. You need to put your video in places where many people can find it and view it. In short, you need to publish your video.

The Biggest and Best: YouTube

The best place to publish your video is where the most people have the best chance of finding it. And that's YouTube.

According to some sources, visitors to YouTube watch more than two billion videos every day. That's "billion" with a big "B"! It is the leading source of online video. And more than 24 hours of new videos are uploaded to the site every minute of every day.

Why does this one service attract the lion's share of online video? First and foremost, it is free, but that alone does not explain it. There are other video hosting sites that are free (which I'll get to later in this chapter).

YouTube makes it easy for people to do a lot of handy things with videos. For example, its powerful search features make it easy for you to find videos on subjects that interest you. And since it's owned by Google, Google does a good job of finding the videos, too.

YouTube also will suggest other videos related to the one that you're watching, which encourages viewers to hang around and watch other videos.

And YouTube makes it easy for people to publish videos. Open a free account, upload your video, and you're done. Once your video is uploaded, you and anyone else can easily get the code needed to either send a link for the video to others in an email, or to embed the video on a Web page so that people can view it there without having to go to the YouTube site.

Needle in a Haystack

If you're paying attention, you should be wishing there was a way to interrupt me and ask a question right about now. If there are 24 *hours* of new videos being uploaded to YouTube *every minute,* how can you expect anyone to find it and watch it? Isn't this just a big waste of time?

That's a good question. And I've got some good answers. First, you have to put the video somewhere so that you can link to it from other places, such as your company Web site or an email newsletter. YouTube is a good choice for this purpose.

But just as important, you can do a lot to make it easy for people to find your video. You can do some very specific things to drive people to your video. These actions center on the concept of keywords.

A keyword is a word that someone might use to search for your company, or for a product or service like the ones that your company offers.

When uploading a new video to YouTube, you can fill in three different types of information about your video: Title, Description, and Tags.

As much as possible, you should work the keywords for your content into all three of these. This will greatly increase your chances of the video being found by people searching for the information that you have in your video.

Let's use our pizza restaurant in Sellersville, Pennsylvania as an example. Let's say that we have decided to create an Attach message (that's the "A" in "PEACH") by creating a video about the Pennridge Rams high school football team. The video shows the restaurant owner delivering a stack of pizzas to the field right after a Friday night game, and includes members of the team talking about the game as they eat the pizza.

This means that we want to work as many of the keywords into the video title as possible. It could be "Pennridge Rams Celebrate Football Win with Sellersville PA Pizza". We'll want to use all those words again in the description, which is a paragraph that describes the video. Finally, we will enter these keywords in the Tags section as individual words separated by spaces. We'll also use any other relevant words that we can think of, such as all the names of towns in the area that are served by the restaurant.

Making good use of keywords in the YouTube video title, description, and tags will help increase the number of people who will find and view your video online.

How Many Viewers?

If you're like most small business owners, you'll want to know as much as you can about who your customers are and where they come from. And if you're like most small business owners, you don't have the time or the budget to spend on finding this out.

One more major advantage of using YouTube to host your online video is that it automatically tracks important data about how many people watch your video. You can access this information by going to your list of Uploaded Videos and clicking on the Insight button for your video.

To illustrate the power of this service, I've used the actual results for a video that I posted about 11 months ago.

The first batch of information lets you see how many viewers have seen your video. As you can see in the illustration, the video has been seen nearly 7,500 times since it was posted. The top graph shows number of views for each day. You can see how the traffic built slowly over the first two months, and then has been more or less steady since then.

Total views of this video: 7,428. In the selected range and region: 995

Show previous: 1 day 7 days 1 month 3 months 6 months 1 year Max

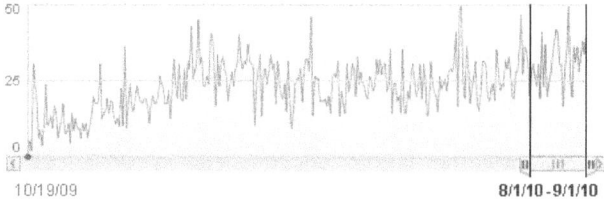

10/19/09   8/1/10 - 9/1/10

Views   How many times has this video been watched?

Daily views ▼   ☐ Show unique users

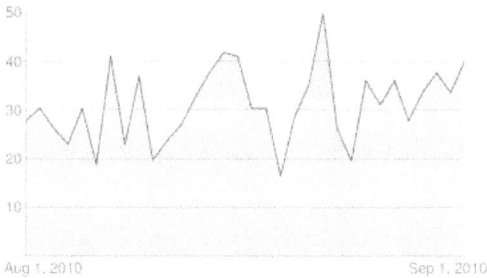

Aug 1, 2010   Sep 1, 2010

YouTube Insight data on video views

You can also take a closer look at the detail for a specific period. The lower graph shows that for the past month, the video has been watched 20 to 40 times a day. If 10% of these views turned into new customers or prospects, what could that mean to your company? Would gaining two to four new customers or prospects per day make a difference in your small business?

This information about the number of views can help you monitor the reception of your video over time. Does it have a spike at the start and then trail off, or does the number of views grow over time as the word spreads about the video and more people watch it? You can also look for spikes that might occur when you get some publicity or run some promotion that might lead to more views.

Links followed to this video	Views	% of total views
YouTube search	2,914	39.4
Related videos	1,988	26.9
Google search	1,030	13.9
No link referrer - YouTube watch and channel pages (?)	517	7.0
External links	295	4.0
No link referrer - mobile devices (?)	281	3.8
No link referrer - embedded player	224	3.0
YouTube other	178	2.4

YouTube Insight data on sending links

You can also see how people came to find your video. In the case of this example, almost 40% found it through a YouTube search. More than a quarter of the people chose to watch it when it was offered as a "related video" when they were watching a different video on YouTube. And about 10% watched the video as the result of a link or embedded video player on some other Web site.

Knowing where people are coming from can tell you a lot. For example, if not many people are coming from other Web sites, then you may not have it presented well on your own Web site. Perhaps there are things you can do to make the video more enticing.

You also will want to know more about the people who are watching your video. This can help you know just who your market is. YouTube Insight has this covered as well.

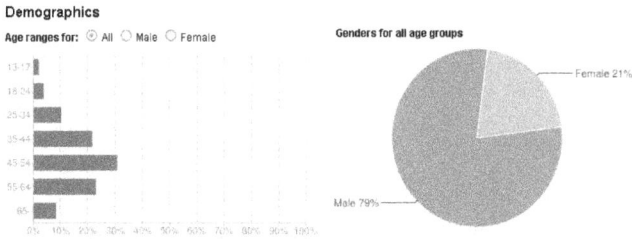

YouTube Insight data on demographics

For the example video, we can see that interest in the video is centered around those who are 45 to 54 years of age. It's also an 80/20 split between men and women.

Perhaps my favorite data of all, however, is the "Hot Spots" results. This tracks how long viewers watch your video. It compares the results to videos of similar length, and shows whether your results are above or below average. A hotter score indicates that fewer people are leaving your video early.

For the sample video, you can see that it has received above average attention from viewers for the first four minutes. (This is why you make sure to cover important content right away in your video, to make sure it gets seen.) The attention tails off in the final minute, and flattens out during the credits.

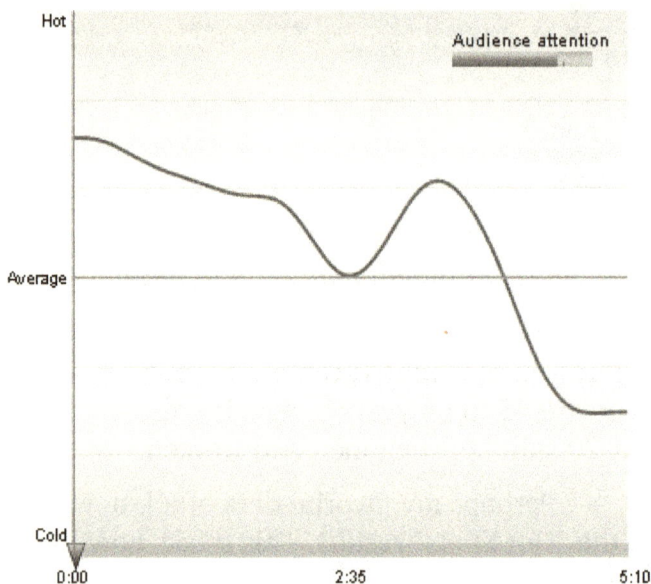

YouTube Insight "Hot Spots" attention statistics

There's a spike around the third minute; it might pay to go see what's different about that portion of the video. I can figure out what is working at that point and repeat that in future videos.

YouTube Insight can tell you a lot about your online video and how well it is working to spread the word about your company's product or service.

Put Your Video on Your Web Site

By now, I hope that I've convinced you to put your video on YouTube. If you're still not sure, let's talk about putting the video on your company Web site.

You could host your video on your Web site's server, but if you should strike gold and it becomes wildly popular, you could use up your bandwidth allocation and run up a big bill with your host service. You don't have that problem when you host it on YouTube.

YouTube also makes it easy to put your video on your Web site. On the YouTube page where you view the video, you can find a Web address (URL) for the video that you can copy and paste into your Web site to create a link to the YouTube page.

You can also find the Web page language (HTML) that lets you embed the video right on your page so that your visitors don't have to leave your site to watch the video. And you don't even have to have a special player installed on your Web site. You can even choose the size of the video window, the color of the surrounding frame, and other settings.

This makes it easy for you (or whoever maintains your Web site) to add the video to your site. And as I described back in Chapter Three, adding the video will improve your company's Web site ranking in Google, helping it rise higher on the list of search results.

Tell Others about Your Video

Next, spread the word. Tell others about your video, because if they like it, they'll tell others about it. They will probably even send along a link to the video. (Has anyone ever sent you a link to an online video that they liked?)

You can email a link to the page on your Web site where the video is embedded. Email this link to your customers, especially if the message has a component that will be of interest to them. Make it part of your response to prospects.

If you have a newsletter—either in print or online—mention your video and provide a link so people can go see it if they want.

Keep in mind that all of these opportunities to mention the video are also an opportunity to deliver the message. As I described back in Chapter Four, you can extract text and images from your video for use online and in print. When you mention the video, be sure to talk about the message that it conveys. Even if the reader never goes and looks at the video, you will have made your point.

Don't forget that you may have other channels open to you to promote the new video. Send out a press release, or at least notify your local papers. Are you part of a Chamber of Commerce? Maybe they will mention the video in the members' news section of their newsletter, or maybe they'll even post a link to the video on their Web site.

Consider other avenues. Does your company belong to any professional or regional organizations? Is there a tie to some other group or organization that might want to show the video on their site or provide a link to it?

All of these opportunities can help you increase the number of people who see your video and are exposed to its message. And when more people see it, more people are likely to mention it to someone they know.

Keep in mind that the benefits can last a long time. Just look back at the daily views that I showed in YouTube Insight. The video has had a fairly steady number of views for the past eight months. You're not going to get that with a single newspaper ad, and probably not even with a Yellow Pages listing.

Just Do It

All of these benefits come from one low-cost and easy step: create an online video. Now, after you've created your first one, creating the next one will be a lot easier. And we'll talk about why you might want to just do it again in the next chapter.

CHAPTER NINE:
LATHER, RINSE, REPEAT

One of the keys to successful marketing is repetition. It helps establish the company's identity and the brand of the product or service. People need repeated exposure to a message before they will be moved to take action.

And remember that Google rewards your Web site for new content. Video content scores even higher than just text, which can help your company rise to the top of the search results. And that's essential if new customers are going to find you.

If people are watching your video and responding to it, it makes sense that you would want to make another video or two. Does this work? Let me tell you about one of the all-star hits of online video.

Will It Blend?

Blendtec is a company that makes industrial-strength blenders for commercial and home applications. I won't say that the product category is duller than dirt, but this clearly is not a product that will get the average person's pulse racing.

Or is it?

The company's founder is Tom Dickson, who does not have a movie star appearance. He's a technology guy who likes to make things that work. He is not someone you'd pick to become a video cult hero.

In 2006, Director of Marketing George Wright created a channel on YouTube and made five videos. The videos showed Dickson in a lab coat and safety glasses feeding unusual objects such as a rake or a handful of marbles into one of the company's blenders, asking the question, "Will it blend?" A minute or two later, he would dump the pulverized results onto the counter; "Yes, it blends!" appears on the screen.

The entire budget for the first five videos was a grand total of $50, not counting the staff time involved.

The second "Will It Blend?" video

Today, there are more than 100 videos in the "Will It Blend?" series that have been viewed for a combined total of more than *135 million times* on YouTube. And that doesn't include the viewers on their Web site at www.willitblend.com.

Was it worth it? Within less than a year from when those first videos were posted, online sales of Blendtec blenders rose 500%. Yes, they were selling five times as many blenders than they had before they posted the videos. Not a bad return on the original $50 investment!

Now, Blendtec is the rock star of online video case studies. The series has become so successful that Nike even *paid* them to blend one of their athletic shoes in a segment. So product placement fees have increased their revenue.

I don't expect anyone reading this book to have that kind of success. It could happen, of course, but I recognize that lightning strikes rarely.

But I also suspect that most people reading this book would be quite happy if they were able to double their sales by using an online video. Even a 10% increase might be sufficient for most people.

But one of the ways to achieve this growth is through repetition. There are many good reasons to create a series of videos for your company's product or service.

Advantages of Repetition

As I just mentioned, adding fresh content to your Web site improves its search engine ranking. Adding video also improves ranking. So adding new video gives you a double dose of good.

A series of videos can do much more than just improve your search ranking, however. It is likely that the people who liked the first video will be interested in seeing a second one in the series. Since people already have an idea what to expect (you've established a relationship of trust with them), they will probably be interested in the next one, too.

If you end up with a series of videos that you post on a consistent schedule, you can even build up a sense of expectation on the part of the viewer. They'll look forward to seeing the next one, which means that they'll be thinking about your company. And that's a good thing.

A series of videos also helps get people talking about them. This can lead to a base of fans who watch and talk about your videos. Word of mouth is the most powerful form of marketing available, so getting people to talk about your videos can have a big impact. Not only will they talk to other fans, but they'll also tell friends and colleagues about it.

An online video can be a pebble thrown in a pond, causing ripples to spread outward. A series of videos can keep those ripples going.

Keys to a Successful Series

Just churning out a lot of videos is not necessarily a recipe for success. If the videos are too much the same, the viewers will lose interest. If they are too different, they won't know what to expect.

The most important aspect of the series is that they have some sort of internal consistency. They don't have to all look the same or cover the same content, but they should deliver similar messages in a similar way.

One step is to use similar graphics for all the videos in a series. Use the same title image, and just change the title text from one to the next. At the end, keep the same closing images, such as a screen that shows the company or product Web site.

By the same token, use the same music. Think of a favorite television show; it probably uses the same opening title sequence and theme music for all its episodes. Repeating the theme music from one video to the next helps create the brand identity and establish the series as a coherent whole.

While the videos need to be similar, they can't be too much alike. If the content is just a rehash of the prior video, your viewers won't be interested. The content for any video in the series must stand on its own. It must be new and fresh compared with the other videos in the series.

It's not that difficult to create a series of videos, no matter which sort of message you have chosen from the PEACH topics. If you're a landscaper showing a property that you've worked on, you can always do another video about another property where you have worked. People who were interested in learning about the first one will probably want to see another one.

Once you've completed your first online video, think about how you can use the new skills and resources you've assembled to create another one.

Online video has the power to boost your marketing efforts with a surprisingly little investment of your time and money. With a little planning, you'll be able to create a video that can help grow your business by attracting new prospects, and strengthening the relationship you have with existing customers.

APPENDIX:

SAMPLE FORMS

Storyboard Template

You can use this storyboard template to plan your video.

Item:	Date Of Shoot:	Location:	Page	Of

	Shot Number:
	Shot Type:
	Action/Script/ Detail:

	Shot Number:
	Shot Type:
	Action/Script/ Detail:

	Shot Number:
	Shot Type:
	Action/Script/ Detail:

	Shot Number:
	Shot Type:
	Action/Script/ Detail:

96

Appearance Release

This is a sample appearance release. You'll need something like this for each person who appears in your online video. This is only offered as an example, and is not intended as legal advice. I encourage you to consult with your lawyer before using any appearance release.

I hereby grant to you, **[your company name here]** (the "Producers") – and their agents, successor or assignees – permission to record my name, likeness, image, voice, sound effects, interview and/or performance on film, tape, still images, or otherwise (the "Recordings"). I grant permission to the Producers to edit such Recordings as they may desire, and incorporate such Recordings into all materials that are developed as a result of this program. The Producers may use and authorize others to use the Recordings, any portions thereof, in all markets, manner and media including but not limited to printed reports, screenings, festivals, educational programs, websites, and broadcast.

It is also understood that any such materials (video, film, photographs, audio, and any other media) will be used with the highest integrity and discretion, with the intent to communicate responsibly and ethically the subject matter contained therein.

Name (please print):
Street address:
City, State, ZIP:
Phone:
Signature:
Date:
Parent or guardian signature (if under 18 years
of age):
Date:

Location Release

*This sample location release is also presented here
as an example, and not as legal advice. You'll
need one of these for any location that is not your
own property. As with the appearance release, I
recommend that you consult with a lawyer before
using a location release.*

Project title:
Production date:

Permission is hereby granted to **[your
company name here]** to use the property
located at **[property address]** for the
purpose of photographing and recording scenes
for the above Project.

Permission includes the right to bring personnel
and equipment onto the property and to
remove them after completion of the work. The
permission herein granted shall include the
right, but not the obligation, to photograph the

actual name(s) connected with the premises and to use such name(s) in the Project.

The undersigned hereby gives to **[your company name here]**, its assigns, agents, licensees, affiliates, clients, principals, and representatives the absolute right and permission to televise, broadcast and distribute, for any lawful purpose, in whole or in part, any scenes containing the above described premises.

Signed:
Date:

TC━F━SB

The Center
for Small Business

The Center for Small Business is dedicated to helping small businesses grow and prosper. We recognize that very small companies have needs that are quite different from those of large corporations. We deliver practical solutions designed to make the most of a company's scarce resources: time and money.

To find out more about The Center and the assistance that it has to offer small businesses, please visit our Web site at www.tcfsb.com.

If you would like to have the author of this book, Alfred Poor, or another representative from The Center deliver a presentation for your organization, please see the Web site or inquire by email to speakers@tcfsb.com for information about program topics and availability.

www.ingramcontent.com/pod-product-compliance
Lightning Source LLC
Chambersburg PA
CBHW022112210326
41521CB00028B/313